POEMS

POEMS

BY

STEPHEN
SPENDER

LONDON
FABER & FABER
24 RUSSELL SQUARE

FIRST PUBLISHED IN MCMXXXIII
BY FABER AND FABER LIMITED
24 RUSSELL SQUARE LONDON W.C. 1
SECOND IMPRESSION MAY MCMXXXIII
SECOND EDITION SEPTEMBER MCMXXXIV
PRINTED IN GREAT BRITAIN BY
R. MACLEHOSE AND COMPANY LIMITED
THE UNIVERSITY PRESS GLASGOW
ALL RIGHTS RESERVED

Inscribed

To CHRISTOPHER ISHERWOOD

CONTENTS

CONTENTS

NOTE

Acknowledgements are due to the editors of the *Criterion*, *Adelphi*, *20th Century*, *New Statesman*, *Listener*, *Spectator*, *New Verse*. Also to the editor of *New Signatures* (the Hogarth Press), and its sequel *New Country*.

I

He will watch the hawk with an indifferent eye
                 Or pitifully;
Nor on those eagles that so feared him, now
                 Will strain his brow;
Weapons men use, stone, sling and strong-thewed
    bow
                 He will not know.

This aristocrat, superb of all instinct,
                 With death close linked
Had paced the enormous cloud, almost had won
                 War on the sun;
Till now, like Icarus mid-ocean-drowned,
                 Hands, wings, are found.

II

R olled over on Europe: the sharp dew frozen to
    stars
Below us: above our heads the night
Frozen again to stars: the stars
In pools between our coats, and that charmed moon:
Ah, what supports? What cross draws out our arms,
Heaves up our bodies towards the wind
And hammers us between the mirrored lights?

Only my body is real: which wolves
Are free to oppress and gnaw. Only this rose
My friend laid on my breast, and these few lines
Written from home, are real.

III

Marston, dropping it in the grate, broke his pipe.
Nothing hung on this act, it was no symbol
Ludicrous for calamity, but merely ludicrous.

That heavy-wrought briar with the great pine face
Now split across like a boxer's hanging dream
Of punishing a nigger, he brought from the con-
    tinent;
It was his absurd relic, like bones,
Of stamping on the white-faced mountains,
Early beds in huts, and other journeys.

To hold the banks of the Danube, the slow barges
    down the river,
Those coracles with faces painted on,
Demanded his last money,
A foodless journey home, as pilgrimage.

IV

Not to you I sighed. No, not a word.
We climbed together. Any feeling was
Formed with the hills. It was like trees' unheard
And monumental sign of country peace.

But next day stumbling, panting up dark stairs,
Rushing in room and door flung wide, I knew.
Oh empty walls, book-carcases, blank chairs
All splintered in my head and cried for you.

V

Acts passed beyond the boundary of mere wishing
Not privy looks, hedged words, at times you saw.
These blundering, heart-surrendered troopers were
Small presents made, and waiting for the tram.
Then once you said 'Waiting was very kind'
And looked surprised: surprising for me too
Whose every movement had been missionary,
 pleading tongue unheard. I had not thought
That you, who nothing else saw, would see this.

So 'very kind' was merest overflow
Something I had not reckoned in myself,
A chance deserter from my force. When we touched
    hands
 felt the whole rebel, feared mutiny
And turned away,
Thinking, if these were tricklings through a dam,
 must have love enough to run a factory on,
Or give a city power, or drive a train.

At the end of two months' holiday there came a
    night
When I lay awake and the sea's distant fretless
    scansion
By imagination scourged rose to a fight
Like the town's roar, pouring out apprehension.
I was in a train. Like the quick spool of a film
I watched hasten away the simple green which can
    heal
All sadness. Abruptly the sign *Ferry to Wilm*
And the cottage by the lake, were vivid, but unreal.
    Real were iron lines, and, smashing the grass
The cars in which we ride, and real our compelled
    time:
Painted on enamel beneath the moving glass
Unreal were cows, the wave-winged storks, the limes
These burned in a clear world from which we pass
Like *rose* and *love* in a forgotten rhyme.

VII

Different living is not living in different places
But creating in the mind a map
Creating in the mind a desert
An isolated mountain or a kinder health-resort.

When I frowned, creating desert, Time only
Shook once his rigid column, as when Ape
Centuries before, with furrowed hand
Grabbed at stone, discerning a new use:
Putting a notch against the mind's progress:
Shaking Time, but with no change of Place.

VIII

An 'I' can never be great man.
This known great one has weakness
To friends is most remarkable for weakness
His ill-temper at meals, his dislike of being con-
    tradicted,
His only real pleasure fishing in ponds,
His only real desire—forgetting.

To advance from friends to the composite self
Central 'I' is surrounded by 'I eating',
'I loving', 'I angry', 'I excreting',
And the 'great I' planted in him
Has nothing to do with all these,

It can never claim its true place
Resting in the forehead, and secure in his gaze.
The 'great I' is an unfortunate intruder
Quarrelling with 'I tiring' and 'I sleeping'
And all those other 'I's who long for 'We dying'.

BEETHOVEN'S DEATH MASK

I imagine him still with heavy brow.
Huge, black, with bent head and falling hair
He ploughs the landscape. His face
Is this hanging mask transfigured,
This mask of death which the white lights make stare.

I see the thick hands clasped; the scare-crow coat;
The light strike upwards at the holes for eyes;
The beast squat in that mouth, whose opening is
The hollow opening of an organ pipe:
There the wind sings and the harsh longing cries.

He moves across my vision like a ship.
What else is iron but he? The fields divide
And, heaving, are changing waters of the sea.
He is prisoned, masked, shut off from being;
Life like a fountain he sees leap—outside.

Yet, in that head there twists the roaring cloud
And coils, as in a shell, the roaring wave.
The damp leaves whisper; bending to the rain
The April rises in him, chokes his lungs
And climbs the torturing passage of his brain.

Then the drums move away, the Distance shows;
Now cloudy peaks are bared; the mystic One
Horizons haze, as the blue incense heaven.
Peace, peace...Then splitting skull and dream, there
    comes,
Blotting our lights, the trumpeter, the sun.

X

Never being, but always at the edge of Being
My head, like Death-mask, is brought into the
     sun.
The shadow pointing finger across cheek,
I move lips for tasting, I move hands for touching,
But never am nearer than touching
Though the spirit lean outward for seeing.
Observing rose, gold, eyes, an admired landscape,
My senses record the act of wishing
Wishing to be
Rose, gold, landscape or another.
I claim fulfilment in the fact of loving.

XI

My parents kept me from children who were
    rough
And who threw words like stones and who wore torn
    clothes.
Their thighs showed through rags. They ran in the
    street
And climbed cliffs and stripped by the country
    streams.

I feared more than tigers their muscles like iron
And their jerking hands and their knees tight on my
    arms.
I feared the salt coarse pointing of those boys
Who copied my lisp behind me on the road.

They were lithe, they sprang out behind hedges
Like dogs to bark at our world. They threw mud
And I looked another way, pretending to smile.
I longed to forgive them, yet they never smiled.

XII

After success, your little afternoon success,
You watch jealous perplexity mould my head
To the shape of a dark and taloned bird
And fix claws in my lungs, and then you pass
Your silk soothing hand across my arm
And smile; I look at you, and through as if through
    glass,
And do not say 'You lie'. There is something in you
Less visible than glass or else it is
A void imagination fills with pities.
You and that famous whore and the thief
Are simple still, I think: you trust belief
Of the lean spectator living on illusion.
This delicate smile that strokes my arm I cannot
Break. It is your truth's invisible creation.

XIII

Alas, when he laughs it is not he:
But a shopwalker who scrapes his hands, and
    bows,
Seller of ties and shirts who shows his teeth
Even out of hours. Sometimes a flickering regret
For these damp, too-generous ruined gestures
Burns in his eyes. If he himself could laugh
To match his light and naked hair
And the jungle still glimmering beneath his lashes,
I think that obdurate cliff
That shuts out all our sky and always grows
Black between us and the silent pools of the will
Would fall: and that the rocks
Would burst with German streams again.

What I expected was
Thunder, fighting,
Long struggles with men
And climbing.
After continual straining
I should grow strong;
Then the rocks would shake
And I should rest long.

What I had not foreseen
Was the gradual day
Weakening the will
Leaking the brightness away,
The lack of good to touch
The fading of body and soul
Like smoke before wind
Corrupt, unsubstantial.

The wearing of Time,
And the watching of cripples pass
With limbs shaped like questions
In their odd twist,
The pulverous grief
Melting the bones with pity,

The sick falling from earth—
These, I could not foresee.

For I had expected always
Some brightness to hold in trust,
Some final innocence
To save from dust;
That, hanging solid,
Would dangle through all
Like the created poem
Or the dazzling crystal.

XV

IN 1929

A whim of Time, the general arbiter,
Proclaims the love instead of death of friends.
Under the domed sky and athletic sun
The three stand naked: the new, bronzed German,
The communist clerk, and myself, being English.

Yet to unwind the travelled sphere twelve years
Then two take arms, spring to a ghostly posture.
Or else roll on the thing a further ten
And this poor clerk with world-offended eyes
Builds with red hands his heaven; makes our bones
The necessary scaffolding to peace.

      ★   ★   ★   ★   ★

Now I suppose that the once-envious dead
Have learnt a strict philosophy of clay
After these centuries, to haunt us no longer
In the churchyard or at the end of the lane
Or howling at the edge of the city
Beyond the last beanrows, near the new factory.

Our fathers killed. And yet there lives no feud
Like prompting Hamlet on the castle stair;

There falls no shade across our blank of peace,
We being together, struck across our path,
Or taper finger threatening solitude.

Our fathers' misery, the dead man's mercy,
The cynic's mystery, weave a philosophy
That the history of man traced purely from dust
Was lipping skulls on the revolving rim
Or the posture of genius with the granite head bowed:

Lives risen a moment, joined or separate,
Fall heavily, then are always separate,
A stratum unreckoned by geologists,
Sod lifted, turned, slapped back again with spade.

XVI

THE PORT

Hopelessly wound round with the cords of street
　　Men wander down their lines of level graves.
Sometimes the maze knots into flaring caves
Where magic-lantern faces skew for greeting.
Smile dawns with a harsh lightning, there's no speak-
　　ing
And, far from lapping laughter, all's parched and
　　hard.
Here the pale lily boys flaunt their bright lips,
Such pretty cups for money, and older whores
Skuttle rat-toothed into the dark outdoors.

Northwards the sea exerts his huge mandate.
His guardians, candles stand, the furnace beam,
Blinking pharos, and ringing from the yards.
In their fat gardens the merchants dwell, South-
　　wards.
Well-fed, well-lit, well-spoken men are these,
With bronze-faced sons, and happy in their
　　daughters.

29

XVII

Moving through the silent crowd
Who stand behind dull cigarettes
These men who idle in the road,
I have the sense of falling light.

They lounge at corners of the street
And greet friends with a shrug of shoulder
And turn their empty pockets out,
The cynical gestures of the poor.

Now they've no work, like better men
Who sit at desks and take much pay
They sleep long nights and rise at ten
To watch the hours that drain away.

I'm jealous of the weeping hours
They stare through with such hungry eyes.
I'm haunted by these images,
I'm haunted by their emptiness.

XVIII

Who live under the shadow of a war,
   What can I do that matters?
My pen stops, and my laughter, dancing, stop
Or ride to a gap.

How often, on the powerful crest of pride,
I am shot with thought
That halts the untamed horses of the blood,
The grip on good.

That moving whimpering and mating bear
Tunes to deaf ears:
Stuffed with the realer passions of the earth
Beneath this hearth.

XIX

Shapes of death haunt life,
  Neurosis eclipsing each in special shadow:
Unrequited love not solving
The need to become another's body
Wears black invisibility:
The greed for property
Heaps a skyscraper over the breathing ribs:
The speedlines of dictators
Cut their own stalks:
From afar, we watch the best of us—
Whose adored desire was to die for the world.

Ambition is my death. That flat thin flame
I feed, that plants my shadow. This prevents love
And offers love of being loved or loving.
The humorous self-forgetful drunkenness
It hates, demands the pyramids
Be built. Who can prevent
His death's industry, which when he sleeps
Throws up its towers? And conceals in slackness
The dreams of revolution, the birth of death?

Also the swallows by autumnal instinct
Comfort us with their effortless exhaustion

32

In great unguided flight to their complete South.
There on my fancied pyramids they lodge
But for delight, their whole compulsion.
Not teaching me to love, but soothing my eyes;
Not saving me from death, but saving me for
     speech.

XX

How strangely this sun reminds me of my love!
Of my walk alone at evening, when like the
cottage smoke
Hope vanished, written amongst red wastes of sky.
I remember my strained listening to his voice
My staring at his face and taking the photograph
With the river behind and the woods touched by
Spring;
Till the identification of a morning—
Expansive sheets of blue rising from fields
Roaring movements of light observed under
shadow—
With his figure leaning over a map, is now complete.

What is left of that smoke which the wind blew away?
I corrupted his confidence and his sunlike happiness
So that even now in his turning of bolts or driving a
machine
His hand will show error. That is for him.
For me this memory which now I behold,
When, from the pasturage, azure rounds me in rings
And the lark ascends, and his voice still rings, still
rings.

XXI

Your body is stars whose million glitter here:
I am lost amongst the branches of this sky
Here near my breast, here in my nostrils, here
Where our vast arms like streams of fire lie.

How can this end? My healing fills the night
And hangs its flags in worlds I cannot near.
Our movements range through miles, and when we
     kiss
The moment widens to enclose long years.

        *   *   *   *   *

Beholders of the promised dawn of truth
The explorers of immense and simple lines,
Here is our goal, men cried, but it was lost
Amongst the mountain mists and mountain pines.

So with this face of love, whose breathings are
A mystery shadowed on the desert floor:
The promise hangs, this swarm of stars and flowers,
And then there comes the shutting of a door.

XXII

FOR T. A. R. H.

Even whilst I watch him I am remembering
The quick laugh of the wasp gold eyes.
The column turning from the staring pane
Even while I see I remember, for love
Is soaked in memory and says
I have seen what I see, and I wear
All pasts and futures like a doomed, domed sky.
Thus I wear always the glint of quick lids
And the blue axel turning; these shall be
Fixed in a night that knows and sees
The equable currents.

At night my life lies with no past nor future
But only space. It watches
Hope and despair and the small vivid longings
Like minnows gnaw the body. Where it drank love
It lives in sameness. Here are
Gestures indelible. The wiry copper hair
And the mothlike lips at dusk and that human
Glance, which makes the sun forgotten.

36

XXIII

THE PRISONERS

Far far the least of all, in want,
  Are these,
The prisoners
Turned massive with their vaults and dark with
    dark.

They raise no hands, which rest upon their knees,
But lean their solid eyes against the night,
Dimly they feel
Only the furniture they use in cells.

Their Time is almost Death. The silted flow
Of years on years
Is marked by dawns
As faint as cracks on mud-flats of despair.

My pity moves amongst them like a breeze
On walls of stone
Fretting for summer leaves, or like a tune
On ears of stone.

Then, when I raise my hands to strike,
It is too late,

There are no chains that fall
Nor visionary liquid door
Melted with anger.

When have their lives been free from walls and dark
And airs that choke?
And where less prisoner to let my anger
Like a sun strike?

If I could follow them from room to womb
To plant some hope
Through the black silk of the big-bellied gown
There would I win.

No, no, no,
It is too late for anger,
Nothing prevails
But pity for the grief they cannot feel.

XXIV

VAN DER LUBBE

O staring eyes, searchlight disks,
Listen at my lips. I am louder than to
Swim an inhuman channel, be boy, or climb
A town's notorious mast.

I throw you these words, I care not which I tear,
You must eat my scraps and dance.
I am glad I am glad that this people is mad:
Their eyes must drink my newspaper glance.

Why do you laugh? Sombre Judge asks.
I laugh at this trial, although it shall make
My life end at a dazzling steel gate,
Axe severing a stalk.

Yes, no, yes, no. Shall I tell you what I know?
Not to Goering, but, dear movietone, I whisper it to
    you.
I laugh because my laughter
Is like justice, twisted by a howitzer.

The senses are shaken from the judging heart:
The eye turned backwards and the outside world

Into the grave of the skull rolled:
With no stars riding heaven, and disparate.

The spitting at justice, the delight of mere guns
Exploding the trees, where in their branches
Truth greenly balances, are what I am
Who die with the dead and slobber with fun.

XXV

Without that once clear aim, the path of flight
 To follow for a life-time through white air,
This century chokes me under roots of night
I suffer like history in Dark Ages, where
Truth lies in dungeons, from which drifts no whisper:
We hear of towers long broken off from sight
And tortures and war, in dark and smoky rumour,
But on men's buried lives there falls no light.
Watch me who walk through coiling streets where
        rain
And fog drown every cry: at corners of day
Road drills explore new areas of pain,
Nor summer nor light may reach down here to play.
The city builds its horror in my brain,
This writing is my only wings away.

XXVI

Passing, men are sorry for the birds in cages
   And for constricted nature hedged and lined,
But what do they say to your pleasant bird
Physical delight, since years tamed?

Behind centuries, behind the continual hill,
The wood you felled, your clothes, the slums you
      built,
Only love knows where that bird dips his head,
Only the sun, soaked in memory, flashes on his neck.

Dance, will you? And sing? Yet pray he is dead,
Invent politics to hide him and law suits and suits:
Now he's impossible and quite destroyed like grass
Where the fields are covered with your more living
      houses.

I never hear you are happy, but I wonder
Whether it was at a shiny bazaar,
At a brittle dance or a party, that you could create
Procrastination of nature, for your talk and laughter
      are
Only a glass that flashes back the light
And that covers only hate.

Will you not forgive him? I have signed his release
Alarming and gentle like the blood's throb,
And his fountain of joy wakes the solitary stag
From his cherished sleep.

But if you still bar your pretty bird, remember
Revenge and despair are prisoned in your bowels.
Life cannot pardon the ideal without scruple,
The enemy of flesh, the angel and destroyer,
Creator of a martyrdom serene, but horrible.

oh young men oh young comrades
it is too late now to stay in those houses
your fathers built where they built you to build to
    breed
money on money   it is too late
to make or even to count what has been made
Count rather those fabulous possessions
which begin with your body and your fiery soul:—
the hairs on your head the muscles extending
in ranges with their lakes across your limbs
Count your eyes as jewels and your valued sex
then count the sun and the innumerable coined light
sparkling on waves and spangled under trees
It is too late to stay in great houses where the ghosts
    are prisoned
—those ladies like flies perfect in amber
those financiers like fossils of bones in coal.
Oh comrades, step beautifully from the solid wall
advance to rebuild and sleep with friend on hill
advance to rebel and remember what you have
no ghost ever had, immured in his hall.

XXVIII

I think continually of those who were truly great.
Who, from the womb, remembered the soul's
   history
Through corridors of light where the hours are suns
Endless and singing. Whose lovely ambition
Was that their lips, still touched with fire,
Should tell of the Spirit clothed from head to foot in
   song.
And who hoarded from the Spring branches
The desires falling across their bodies like blossoms.

What is precious is never to forget
The essential delight of the blood drawn from ageless
   springs
Breaking through rocks in worlds before our earth.
Never to deny its pleasure in the morning simple
   light
Nor its grave evening demand for love.
Never to allow gradually the traffic to smother
With noise and fog the flowering of the spirit.

Near the snow, near the sun, in the highest fields
See how these names are fêted by the waving grass

45

And by the streamers of white cloud
And whispers of wind in the listening sky.
The names of those who in their lives fought for life
Who wore at their hearts the fire's centre.
Born of the sun they travelled a short while towards
    the sun,
And left the vivid air signed with their honour.

XXIX

After they have tired of the brilliance of cities
   And of striving for office where at last they may
      languish
Hung round with easy chains until
Death and Jerusalem glorify also the crossing-
      sweeper:
Then those streets the rich built and their easy love
Fade like old cloths, and it is death stalks through
      life
Grinning white through all faces
Clean and equal like the shine from snow.

In this time when grief pours freezing over us,
When the hard light of pain gleams at every street
      corner,
When those who were pillars of that day's gold roof
Shrink in their clothes; surely from hunger
We may strike fire, like fire from flint? ·
And our strength is now the strength of our bones
Clean and equal like the shine from snow
And the strength of famine and of our enforced idle-
      ness,
And it is the strength of our love for each other.

Readers of this strange language,
We have come at last to a country
Where light equal, like the shine from snow, strikes
    all faces,
Here you may wonder
How it was that works, money, interest, building,
    could ever hide
The palpable and obvious love of man for man.

Oh comrades, let not those who follow after
—The beautiful generation that shall spring from
    our sides—
Let not them wonder how after the failure of banks
The failure of cathedrals and the declared insanity
    of our rulers,
We lacked the Spring-like resources of the tiger
Or of plants who strike out new roots to gushing
    waters.
But through torn-down portions of old fabric let
    their eyes
Watch the admiring dawn explode like a shell
Around us, dazing us with its light like snow.

XXX

PERHAPS

The explosion of a bomb
  the submarine—a burst bubble filled with
    water—
the chancellor clutching his shot arm (and that was
    Perhaps
a put-up job for their own photographers)
the parliament their own side set afire
and then our party forbidden
and the mine flooded, an accident I hope.

motorcycles wires aeroplanes cars trains
converging at that one town Geneva
top-hats talking at edge of crystal healing lake
then mountains.

We know this from rotating machines
from flanges stamping, cutting, sicking out sheets
              from paper rolls.
The newsmen run like points of compass: their arms
    are
gusts that carry sheets of mouldy paper:
our eyes mud those scraps rub on.

D   49

In his skidding car he wonders
when watching landscape attack him
'is it rushing (I cannot grasp it) or is it
at rest with its own silence I cannot touch?'

Was that final when they shot him? did that war
lop our dead branches? are my new leaves splendid?
is it leviathan, that revolution
hugely nosing at edge of antarctic?

only Perhaps. Can be that we grow smaller
donnish and bony shut in our racing prison:
headlines are walls that shake and close
the dry dice rattled in their wooden box.

Can be deception of things only changing. Out there
perhaps growth of humanity above the plain
hangs: not the timed explosion, oh but Time
monstrous with stillness like the himalayan range.

XXXI

THE FUNERAL

Death is another milestone on their way.
With laughter on their lips and with winds blow-
    ing round them
They record simply
How this one excelled all others in making driving
    belts.

This is festivity, it is the time of statistics
When they record what one unit contributed:
They are glad as they lay him back in the earth
And thank him for what he gave them.

They walk home remembering the straining red flags,
And with pennons of song still fluttering through
    their blood
They speak of the world state
With its towns like brain-centres and its pulsing
    arteries.

They think how one life hums, revolves and toils,
One cog in a golden and singing hive:
Like spark from fire, its task happily achieved,
It falls away quietly.

No more are they haunted by the individual grief
Nor the crocodile tears of European genius,
The decline of a culture
Mourned by scholars who dream of the ghosts of
    Greek boys.

XXXII

THE EXPRESS

After the first powerful plain manifesto
The black statement of pistons, without more fuss
But gliding like a queen, she leaves the station.
Without bowing and with restrained unconcern
She passes the houses which humbly crowd outside,
The gasworks and at last the heavy page
Of death, printed by gravestones in the cemetery.
Beyond the town there lies the open country
Where, gathering speed, she acquires mystery,
The luminous self-possession of ships on ocean.
It is now she begins to sing—at first quite low
Then loud, and at last with a jazzy madness—
The song of her whistle screaming at curves,
Of deafening tunnels, brakes, innumerable bolts.
And always light, aerial, underneath
Goes the elate metre of her wheels.
Steaming through metal landscape on her lines
She plunges new eras of wild happiness
Where speed throws up strange shapes, broad curves
And parallels clean like the steel of guns.
At last, further than Edinburgh or Rome,
Beyond the crest of the world, she reaches night

Where only a low streamline brightness
Of phosphorus on the tossing hills is white.
Ah, like a comet through flame she moves entranced
Wrapt in her music no bird song, no, nor bough
Breaking with honey buds, shall ever equal.

XXXIII

THE LANDSCAPE NEAR AN AERODROME

More beautiful and soft than any moth
    With burring furred antennae feeling its huge
    path
Through dusk, the air-liner with shut-off engines
Glides over suburbs and the sleeves set trailing tall
To point the wind. Gently, broadly, she falls
Scarcely disturbing charted currents of air.

Lulled by descent, the travellers across sea
And across feminine land indulging its easy limbs
In miles of softness, now let their eyes trained by
    watching
Penetrate through dusk the outskirts of this town
Here where industry shows a fraying edge.
Here they may see what is being done.

Beyond the winking masthead light
And the landing-ground, they observe the outposts
Of work: chimneys like lank black fingers
Or figures frightening and mad: and squat buildings
With their strange air behind trees, like women's
    faces

Shattered by grief. Here where few houses
Moan with faint light behind their blinds
They remark the unhomely sense of complaint, like
    a dog
Shut out and shivering at the foreign moon.

In the last sweep of love, they pass over fields
Behind the aerodrome, where boys play all day
Hacking dead grass: whose cries, like wild birds,
Settle upon the nearest roofs
But soon are hid under the loud city.

Then, as they land, they hear the tolling bell
Reaching across the landscape of hysteria
To where, larger than all the charcoaled batteries
And imaged towers against that dying sky,
Religion stands, the church blocking the sun.

XXXIV

THE PYLONS

The secret of these hills was stone, and cottages
  Of that stone made,
And crumbling roads
That turned on sudden hidden villages.

Now over these small hills they have built the con-
  crete
That trails black wire:
Pylons, those pillars
Bare like nude, giant girls that have no secret.

The valley with its gilt and evening look
And the green chestnut
Of customary root
Are mocked dry like the parched bed of a brook.

But far above and far as sight endures
Like whips of anger
With lightning's danger
There runs the quick perspective of the future.

This dwarfs our emerald country by its trek
So tall with prophecy:
Dreaming of cities
Where often clouds shall lean their swan-white neck.

XXXV

Abrupt and charming mover,
Your pointed eyes under lit leaves,
Your light hair, your smile,
I watch burn in a land
Bright in the cave of night
And protected by my hand.

Beneath the ribs, in Jonah's whale,
All night I hold you: from day
I have recalled your play
Disturbing as birds' flying
And with the Spring's infection
And denial of satisfaction.

You dance, forgetting all: in joy
Sustaining that instant of the eye
Which like a flaming wheel can be:
Your games of cards, hockey with toughs,
Winking at girls, shoes cribbed from toffs,
Like the encircling summer dew
Glaze me from head to toe.

By night I hold you, but by day
I watch you weave the silk cocoon
Of a son's, or a skater's, play:

We have no meeting place
Beneath that dancing, glassy surface:
The outward figure of delight
Creates no warm and sanguine image
Answering my language.

XXXVI

In railway halls, on pavements near the traffic,
They beg, their eyes made big by empty staring
And only measuring Time, like the blank clock.

No, I shall weave no tracery of pen-ornament
To make them birds upon my singing-tree:
Time merely drives these lives which do not live
As tides push rotten stuff along the shore.

—There is no consolation, no, none
In the curving beauty of that line
Traced on our graphs through history, where the
    oppressor
Starves and deprives the poor.

Paint here no draped despairs, no saddening clouds
Where the soul rests, proclaims eternity.
But let the wrong cry out as raw as wounds
This Time forgets and never heals, far less transcends.

61

XXXVII

Those fireballs, those ashes,
    Those cloudbursts, those whirling madman hurri-
    canes
The palatial sky breathes, make men's organic
    change.
Some, extinguished by horror, leap into the thinnest
    air,
Inevitable delight is theirs, no sweeter delight
Than to be keener than knives, invisible to run
Around the endless earth, for ever to blow upon
The lips of their loved friends.
Others shake in bed whilst the sorrowing elements
Twist them to shapes of dreadful grief,
Only the mirror knows their traitorous joy.
Man must rejoice, misfortune cannot fall,
Him I delight in accepts joy as joy;
He is richened by sorrow as a river by its bends,
He is the swallower of fire,
His bowels are molten fire; when he leaves his friend
He takes pleasure in icy solitude; he is the dandy;
He is the swimmer, waves only lift him higher,
He is the rose, sultry loveliness does not oppress him;
The clouds of our obscuring disillusion

Are thoughts which shade his brow, and then he
    smiles.
I stand far from him, but I wish that these
Slanting iron hail pattern no stigmata
Showing me sadder than those poor, and rarer.
Let the elements that fall make me of finer mixture
Not struck from sorrow, but vast joys, and learning
    laughter.

XXXVIII

NEW YEAR

Here at the centre of the turning year,
The turning Polar North,
The frozen streets, and the black fiery joy
Of the Child launched again forth,
I ask that all the years and years
Of future disappointment, like a snow
Chide me at one fall now.

I leave him who burns endlessly
In the brandy pudding crowned with holly,
And I ask that Time should freeze my skin
And all my fellow travellers harden
Who are not flattered by this town
Nor up its twenty storeys whirled
To prostitutes without infection.

Cloak us in accidents and in the failure
Of the high altar and marital adventure;
In family disgrace, denunciation
Of bankers, a premier's assassination.
From the government windows
Let heads of headlines watch depart,
Strangely depart by staying, those
Who build a new world in their heart.

Where scythe shall curve but not upon our neck
And lovers proceed to their forgetting work,
Answering the harvests of obliteration.
After the frozen years and streets
Our tempered will shall plough across the nations.
The engine hurrying through the lucky valley
The hand that moves to guide the silent lines
Effect their beauty without robbery.

XXXIX

From all these events, from the slump, from the
    war, from the boom,
From the Italian holiday, from the skirring
Of the revolving light for an adventurer,
From the crowds in the square at dusk, from the
    shooting,
From the loving, from the dying, however we pros-
    per in death
Whether lying under twin lilies and branched candles
Or stiffened on the pavement like a frozen sack,
    hidden
From night and peace by the lamps:
From all these events, Time solitary will emerge
Like a rocket bursting from mist: above the trouble
Untangled with our pasts, be sure Time will leave us.

At first growing up in us more nakedly than our own
    nature
Driving us beyond what seemed the final choking
    swamp,
Ruin, the all-covering illness, to a new and empty
    air;
Singling us from the war which killed ten millions;

Carrying us elate through the happy summer fields;
Nesting us in high rooms of a house where voices
Murmured at night from the garden, as if flowering
    from water;
Then sending us to lean days after the years of fulfil-
    ment;
At last dropping us into the hard, bright crater of
    the dead.

Our universal ally, but larger than our purpose,
    whose flanks
Stretch to planets unknown in our brief, particular
    battle,
Tomorrow Time's progress will forget us even here,
When our bodies are rejected like the beetle's shard,
    today
Already, now, we are forgotten on those stellar shores.
Time's ambition, huge as space, will hang its flags
In distant worlds, and in years on this world as dis-
    tant.

XL

Not palaces, an era's crown
 Where the mind dwells, intrigues, rests;
The architectural gold-leaved flower
From people ordered like a single mind,
I build. This only what I tell:
It is too late for rare accumulation
For family pride, for beauty's filtered dusts;
I say, stamping the words with emphasis,
Drink from here energy and only energy,
As from the electric charge of a battery,
To will this Time's change.
Eye, gazelle, delicate wanderer,
Drinker of horizon's fluid line;
Ear that suspends on a chord
The spirit drinking timelessness;
Touch, love, all senses;
Leave your gardens, your singing feasts,
Your dreams of suns circling before our sun,
Of heaven after our world.
Instead, watch images of flashing brass
That strike the outward sense, the polished will
Flag of our purpose which the wind engraves.

68

No spirit seek here rest. But this: No man
Shall hunger: Man shall spend equally.
Our goal which we compel: Man shall be man.

—That programme of the antique Satan
Bristling with guns on the indented page
With battleship towering from hilly waves:
For what? Drive of a ruining purpose
Destroying all but its age-long exploiters.
Our programme like this, yet opposite,
Death to the killers, bringing light to life.